Fire When
They Talk

FIRE WHEN THEY TALK

Ivy Forest

Columbus, Ohio

The views and opinions expressed in this book are solely those of the author and do not reflect the views or opinions of Gatekeeper Press. Gatekeeper Press is not to be held responsible for and expressly disclaims responsibility of the content herein.

Fire When They Talk

Published by Gatekeeper Press

2167 Stringtown Rd, Suite 109

Columbus, OH 43123-2989

www.GatekeeperPress.com

Copyright © 2022 by Ivy Forest

All rights reserved. Neither this book, nor any parts within it may be sold or reproduced in any form or by any electronic or mechanical means, including information storage and retrieval systems, without permission in writing from the author. The only exception is by a reviewer, who may quote short excerpts in a review.

The cover design, interior formatting, typesetting, and editorial work for this book are entirely the product of the author. Gatekeeper Press did not participate in and is not responsible for any aspect of these elements.

Library of Congress Control Number: 2022936893

ISBN (paperback): 9781662927317

Contents

PART ONE
FIRE 1

The First Thanksgiving	5
Christmas In Oklahoma	7
Returning Home From The Holiday	10
Self Harm to Get a Word In	14
The Bonobo Concert	17
New Orleans	22
The Road Trip From Oklahoma	24
Road Trip Number 2. You Really are the Worst Traveller	28
Astral Connection	31
At a Stoplight	33
It Wasn't The Dog	35
It Started Out Consensual	37
Lunch With Sam	39
Where'd You Hide My Drugs	40
Destroying My Sister's Paintings	46
Pit Stop In New Mexico	49
Tom's Cabin	51
The First Time I Said "I Hate You"	53
Swerving Toward a Man on a Bike	57
Down Low At Lowdown	59
Unwillingly Having Sex With You To Maintain This Relationship	61

When I Found Your Relationship Journal	63
The Night of Crush Walls	67
Butts And Trumpets	69
The Last Time I Saw You	71

PART TWO
WATER — 75

Normalize Love	77
Strangers to Neighbors	79
Reverse Pick-Pocket	81
Heather Love	83
The World Shows Me Its Secrets Because It Knows I Can Keep Them	85
Strange Woman In A Strange Land	87
Pacing Wires	90
Not a Match	91
Ali	92
Reza	94
Mauricio	96
Turbulence	101
New Years In Guadalajara	103
Damien	105
Parental Supervision	109

Dedications:

To Courtney, my dear friend since fifth grade. We've watched each other grow from childhood, through adolescence, and into adulthood. Through the best and worst times you've been there. You're the first friend I had that moved far away, and taught me the most valuable lesson of letting go. I remember every moment we've ever shared and I can't wait to create more memories with you.

To my mother, for always believing in me.

To my father, for inspiring me to do everything I've ever wanted and to not be afraid of what anyone thinks.

To John, for loving me unconditionally even though I'm not his biological child. And for loving my mother in the best way possible.

PART ONE

FIRE

This book is a collection of short stories that focus on a toxic relationship, and highlights the love experienced outside of romantic relationships; including fleeting moments, friends that I've had throughout the years, and people I've met on vacation. It encompasses the idea that people don't need a romantic relationship to experience true love. After years of working through my trauma and talking to other people about their previous relationships, I realized that far too often people are trapped in an abusive partnership.

Most relationships refer to romantic partners, but some can be friends, and more often than not, family members. It's hard to say why exactly we stay in relationships that are emotionally and sometimes physically abusive.

My personal excuse, was due to the fact that my mental state significantly declined. I was constantly fatigued from arguing and crying. I wasn't able to maintain a full time job schedule. I'd lived with my partner at the time in their studio, rent-free. If I spent more hours at work, they'd get anxious. I'd constantly have to check in with them, and what was only a part time job began to feel like over time.

I'd even suggested getting my own place with a roommate, but they were weary of that idea and said no. They constantly held the fact that they provided me with housing over my head.

Hanging out with friends alone rarely ever happened and when it did, a fight always ensued when

I returned home. I couldn't be with friends or family alone. Wasn't able to fly out to visit any of them unless he tagged along. Isolating me from them, harassing me at work, and constantly ensuring my avenues of escape were always narrow.

My life began after the relationship was over. The two years we spent together was similar to what a cold-blooded animal experiences during brumation.

Love is around us-- everywhere, and we aren't alone because of it. I think we can benefit from the idea that the qualities we're searching for in a romantic partner won't often be found in a single person. We can have friends that embody the qualities we're most fond of. The archaic idea that there's someone out there for everyone, with the exact traits and ideals we seek is an improbable notion. In the short time we have on this Earth, we should welcome platonic relationships with a sizeable embrace.

Too often people lose themselves within romantic relationships and misplace their sense of individuality. The person in the mirror becomes only a shadow of our former selves. When escaping a toxic partnership, people tend to feel the same way; like they've lost an integral part of their inner being. The feeling of loss can linger for months or years, and it takes an immense amount of time to realize what you thought would be an abysmal decision, turns out to be an efflorescence of our future identity. It teaches us boundaries and shows us what we can and won't accept in our lives.

The First Thanksgiving

We woke up around noon. I'd felt dizzy all morning and was running a fever. I was slowly getting ready to go to your parent's house. You were bumbling around anxiously as usual. I let you know I wasn't feeling well and your response was: "People are only as sick as they want to be." I decided then I was going to power through. And praying to anything and everything out there that I got even sicker.

I decided my wardrobe that day should mimic how I was feeling. I settled on jeans and a grey hoodie.

You give me a once-over and say "I don't know how your family does holidays, but I expect you to dress a little nicer when we go to my parent's."

I disassociated. I can't even remember what I'd changed into next.

We arrive at your parents' house and go through the motions. The football game. The praying. The dinner.

Still running a fever and shoveling hot turkey and gravy down my throat.

15 minutes into dinner I can feel it's finally happening. This is what I've been spitefully waiting for all day.

The wave of nausea feeling similar to an orgasm at this point.

Now I can prove to you I was actually sick. I wasn't just trying to get out of visiting your family.

I abruptly leave the table and run to the bathroom, door open, and start puking.

Your niece comes to the door to ask if I'm okay and I hear you say "She's fine" and I hear you repeat the same lines from earlier "She's only sick because she wants to be".

I continue puking and I hear your mother spraying Lysol around the house.

The emotion I felt when I left the bathroom was victorious. I SHOWED you how sick I actually was. I didn't choose this. and I SHOWED your family what an uncaring, insensitive prick you were. At least I'd thought so. I think they're so used to it they don't even think twice about it anymore. It's a shame none of them told you to be more understanding. Maybe hatred runs in the family.

Christmas In Oklahoma

At the crowded airport headed to security, you were already in a bad mood. A TSA worker directs us downstairs-the opposite direction in which we were heading. They told us south security was shorter.

You rolled your eyes and muttered obscenities under your breath. We make it downstairs and stand in the long line.

The entire 30 minutes we stood there you kept looking back up at the TSA worker saying "Fuck that guy" For some reason you thought we were in the longer line and the TSA worker made a personal attack on us by directing us to South security.

You wouldn't stop complaining.

I kept quiet as long as I could. I knew if I said anything to disagree with you, we'd start fighting. If I joined in with you, it would only make your mood worse.

STILL complaining, you have nothing else to say but negative words.

It's a fucking line at the airport during the holidays.

What did you expect?

I couldn't take it anymore and in a hushed tone I finally said "Yeah I get it, you keep repeating yourself"

I knew then I'd just ruined the whole day.

I just wanted you to stop and I said it as nice as I could.

You ignored me through security. Through the flight you were pouting and fell asleep.

When the plane lands your eyes pop open.

You woke up and chose violence.

Again, the first words out of your mouth are negative comments. Comments about people standing up too quick. Not moving quickly enough.

Why are you always in such a hurry? In such a bad mood?

I stay silent because last time I opened my mouth it made you even angrier. This time though you got mad because I didn't say anything. We didn't even make it off the plane and we've already launched another fight.

I said I wasn't going to fight in front of my parents— they were waiting at baggage claim for us.

Oh how that statement seemed to fill you with rage.

When we got off the jet bridge you walked quickly ahead of me, stomping angrily and bobbing and weaving through everyone. I tried to catch up with you.

I wanted to make sure we seemed normal by the time we walked up to my parents.

I caught up to you and grabbed your arm and you hastily yanked it away from me.

You had that look on your face. The one that I HATE. The one that instills fear and disgust in me at the same time.

You kept that look on your face even as we were approaching baggage claim. Whenever I see that look I want to peel it right off your face with a vegetable peeler. You kept that glare as you death marched right past my mother. She looks over at me and I can tell she's concerned. Holding back tears I whispered to her that I hated you.

When we both met you at baggage claim you decided to act right again. Even though my mom clearly noticed your hostile character.

You're such a phony, hateful, ignorant, inflictor of agony.

Returning Home From The Holiday

The holiday started out pretty okay. Maybe you were on your best behavior because it was my birthday. We took an iconic polaroid photo of us that eerily captured the fleeting moments of our happiness. I still have it.

Things seemed to be smoothed over from our initial arrival. But here we are at the airport again. On our way home to Denver. We make it to the gate and see the flight's been delayed due to weather. You suggest grabbing a drink at the bar just around the corner from the gate. We sit down and order greyhounds. Our signature drink.

After the first drink you seemed calmer. We were watching the flight schedule behind us. Apparently the flight was delayed even further. We were checking back every so often. You decided we should have another drink. And then another. We were having a good moment. I'd been waiting for one of these.

We hadn't heard any announcements and since we were finished drinking, we decided to head to our gate.

We arrive there and they're boarding for a flight to San Diego. They must've switched the gate.

We ask a person next to us if they were waiting for the flight back to Denver. They informed us the flight had left 30 minutes prior.

My heart sank.

This was going to send us back to where we began our trip.

Here you go again, storming off and cursing. Except you weren't cursing under your breath this time. You were cursing at an alarming volume. Over and over like a broken record all you kept saying was Fuck --- and Fucking---- Fuck----

I was spellbound by your insanity.

We make it to the airline help desk and you're cursing at the workers. Saying it was their fault we'd missed our flight. This was actually all your fault.

The worker let us know there wasn't another flight out to Denver for the next couple of days.

You stormed off from the desk and started screaming again. Literally screaming in a public place as I begged you to stop.

I was embarrassed.

Mostly just scared.

How can I love someone, fear them, and be so utterly disgusted by the person all at once?

You were manic, with the wild look of the devil in your eyes.

I don't even believe in the devil, but he exists in you.

Still cursing and screaming, walking in circles in the airport, we're approached by a police officer.

"Everything alright here, folks?"

God. This is gonna be it. You're gonna get arrested. I'll have to explain to my family what happened. And you're gonna be locked away.

I was simultaneously scared and hopeful.

Hopefully you'd get taken away and maybe then you'd see that how you behave just isn't acceptable.

You surprised me. You actually gathered yourself. Why is it you only act with decency around figures of authority?

I call my family and lie to them. I tell them we got held up in security and we didn't make it to our gate in time. Tell them we missed the flight and left out all of your nasty details.

You weren't appreciative when they picked us up.

You didn't say thank you.

When they offered to pay for our flights back home you were hateful. Snappy.

They bought them anyway and you mustered a pouty, pathetic little thank you.

You sicken me.

Self Harm to Get a Word In

This story is the one where you like to put all the blame on me. You like to say this is where our toxic habits were born.

The week before we'd had a conversation about being in an open relationship.

We'd talked about our previous relationships being open.

We'd come to an agreement that we'd give it a try ourselves.

You invited one of your old girlfriends over to my apartment. You spent the night talking with her. She talked about the couple she was currently dating.

The next night you'd told me you were going out with your friend Lauren. That's fine with me. You message me rather late that night.

Letting me know you'd been out with her late.

I'd had someone over as well but you came over the next day.

After you and I hooked up, you immediately called planned parenthood; while I was in the room and said you needed to get an STD test.

A pause.

You answered the person over the phone with: "In the past month? Probably about 5 sexual partners."

You made an appointment.

Your attitude changed after this and I could sense it.

I mentioned to you that I was going to visit my (male friend) over Christmas.

You admitted your feelings for me right then and gave me an ultimatum.

You mentioned it was either him or you.

You told me that the "Open Relationship" nonsense was my plan, and that I had commitment issues.

I countered your argument with the fact that we'd BOTH agreed on this. We BOTH shared our past with open relationships.

You also spent the night with another woman. You brought one of your exes over. And I'd been nothing but open.

You threw this back in my face trying to put all the blame on me. I believe its called GASLIGHTING.

Arguing back and forth in my living room, you completely diminish my voice by screaming over me. Asking me questions in a furious tone. Not even giving me the chance to answer.

This was the first time. I didn't know what else to do. I'd been trying to talk. Calmly. Let you know how I was feeling. And you kept yelling.

That's the first time. The first time I struck myself in the face. One hard hit from myself across the cheek and you finally stopped talking.

I felt RELIEF. FINALLY. Another 3 strikes to my own face, and then you have your eyes on me. You're silent. And now I can finally speak. This makes you listen. I've cracked the code. Perfect.

One scenario of many. But this was the first.

The Bonobo Concert

I was looking forward to this.

We went together and met up with a couple of your friends.

The show started and we got a couple of beers.

The show continues. We're swaying, doing little dances, smoking weed.

The show ends.

Walking down the ramp headed back to the parking lot you really let the hate flow through you.

Talking loudly as usual, the ENTIRE way back to the car—and it's a long trek.

Over and over you kept saying: "What the fuck was that? That shit was so slow. Such a downer. I've been to other shows of theirs and this is the shittiest one. I can't believe we paid for this."

Embarrassment settles into my bones once again.

You're so rude.

Everyone within 5 feet of us can hear you going off.

Even your friends weren't joining in on your rant.

You look over to me and say "What? It SUCKED and I'm ALLOWED to say that."

Okay. Sure.

We get in the car and I'm dreading the 45 minute drive home.

We were in my jeep.

Of course we start arguing. What's a Friday night out without a good old-fashioned argument between the two of us?

Instigated by you, of course.

I recorded the audio of this fight on my phone.

I wanted proof of how you sound during fights like this.

I could tell this was yet another scenario where you'd be blacking out.

Screaming at the top of your lungs. Interrupting me. Talking over me. The works.

I had to stop at a gas station on the way back home and fill up. You'd had the window rolled down and continued to scream at me while I was filling up.

Trying my hardest to tune you out, the sharpest words I could hear pouring out of your evil, sick mouth were "FUCK" and "FUCKING" and "GOD DAMNIT" and phrases like "YOU ALWAYS" and "YOU NEVER."

You puke out the window.

Fire When They Talk

This is becoming a situation now and people are staring.

As they usually do when a domestic dispute occurs in public.

You open the door completely and puke some more.

The funny thing is, even though you're vomiting, you still find it necessary to continue screaming at me between hurls.

I say "SHH" and "Shut the fuck up, people are staring, they're gonna call the police."

Those words certainly didn't influence you to get your shit together.

You slam my door shut and continue going off.

I rolled your window up and start heading home and of course the argument continues.

You're pounding your fists on my door handle over and over and over.

Still recording. This is gold.

Now you'll finally understand that it's YOU that takes these situations over the top.

The next morning?

Sunlight reveals he'd actually permanently damaged my door handle. The automatic window buttons were all out of place.

Thanks.

You offered to pay for the damage but you never did.

That same morning, making sure you'd eaten and had your daily dose of marijuana so you could function somewhat as a normal human being, I decided it was time to show you the recording.

I expected you to be apologetic; shocked even, for the way you speak to me. Shocked at the things you say to me.

I just couldn't believe that you'd intentionally treat me this way. This was the excuse I created for you.

It was my assumption that you didn't know what you were doing when you were treating me this way. Almost like you'd dissociate and then treat me so awfully.

You weren't sorry.

You got angry.

You didn't like what you heard but it was wrong of me to record you. You said it was conniving of me to do something like that.

I betrayed you by recording you in a drunken rage, providing you with the evidence to let you know I'm not crazy.

To let you know I'm not overreacting when I say you treat me like shit.

You walked away from me and didn't say sorry for anything.

It's like you were proud of the spiteful things you said.

New Orleans

I'd never been here before. It was our first trip together as a couple.

Surely you'd be completely relaxed on vacation.

After check-in we decided to venture out and go for a walk. See where we ended up in the city.

Within 15 minutes of walking you start getting frustrated. Cursing about how you can't read a fucking map.

Walking fast, ahead of me.

When you "figured out" where you were the attitude dropped.

Maybe it's because we'd just found the nearest bar and you needed a drink.

Sitting at the bar you're hyping me up about the best places to eat and the culture here in New Orleans. We were planning all the things we'd wanted to do.

But since we'd been in Louisiana for about an hour and you've already thrown a tantrum, I had my doubts.

You went to the restroom.

On the bar there was a clear glass jar with plain white matchbooks.

I plowed my hand through the mouth of the jar and pulled out a single matchbook.

Opened the cover, exposing a lineup of red tipped matches.

Inside the cover was a hand-written note.

In pencil.

It read: "Remember, it always gets better"

I hope so.

I held onto this the entire trip.

Also throughout our entire relationship.

The remainder of the trip?

Hot and cold.

Actually, let's say psychotic and tolerable.

We'd gone to one of those above ground cemeteries. You had me film you in your bird mask. You were going to use this footage for a music video.

You got angry with me because I wasn't holding the camera correctly. Getting the right shots. Taking your orders with a smile on my face as you barked them at me.

I was no longer your girlfriend.

I became an assistant to the biggest narcissist I've ever known.

A truly unbearable experience.

The Road Trip From Oklahoma

We'd been visiting for the fourth of July.

I'd really been missing my family and overall, we had a pretty normal trip.

As soon as we packed up, loaded the car, and drove five minutes down the road, the fighting continues.

We'd just left, it would've taken less than five minutes to go back to my family's house.

On the road I realize I don't have my wallet so I politely ask you to pull over so I can look for it.

Immediately your face changes.

Your callous tone makes its grand entry.

On the side of the road now I start rifling through my bags and you start insulting me.

"You always do this, you always forget your fucking shit."

We were yelling back and forth when a white car pulls up behind us.

It's my sister. She saw us fighting on the side of the road and wanted to make sure we were okay.

You didn't say anything. Just looked away.

We got back in the car and started driving down the road.

You continued going off on me.

10 more hours of driving.

Hopefully we got the worst part of it out of the way.

Wishful thinking on my part.

About halfway through the rest of the drive home you'd gotten a call from the fire marshal.

Apparently they reported you for having squatters in the basement of the shop.

Arguing back and forth with the fire marshal over the phone I start tensing up.

This is getting heated.

Finally the call is over and you start screaming and hitting the dashboard.

I can't take it when you're like this.

I hate this existence.

Still yelling, you're not taking any of the responsibility.

You blame the people in the basement for "blowing your cover" and for "destroying the empire that you created"

Relax.

Your parents own the majority of the business.

You didn't build shit.

I can't take it anymore and try deescalating the situation.

I'm aware this is going to be another failed attempt at calming you down.

You kept insulting me. Telling me I didn't have shit. I'm too young to understand.

Now we're really going at it. Now I'm heated too. Your hate spilled over into me.

Still yelling, you start angrily swerving back and forth.

Slinging one insult after another.

I'm throwing them right back. Telling you you're toxic. Telling you that I had nothing to do with this situation and said I didn't deserve this.

I'm crying now.

That's when you yelled "WELL FUCK ME, I GUESS I JUST HAVE FOOT IN MOUTH SYNDROME"

Then you take both hands off the wheel, take your seatbelt off, and bring your foot up to your face and literally put it in your mouth.

Still screaming I have to steady the wheel. I'm telling you to pull over, pull over, PULL THE FUCK OVER.

Finally you do.

You get out of the car without saying anything.

You rip your shirt off and start screaming as loud as you can. Pacing up and down the road for the next 15 minutes.

All I hear is cursing.

What should've been a 10 hour car ride turned into 12 hours because of your outburst and little detour.

10 years older than me yet you act like such a child.

You're a disgrace.

After nearly killing us on the road I have to keep it together.

My survival depends on it.

This has become a hostage situation.

I stay as silent. Obedient. And as complacent as you need me to be.

Road Trip Number 2. You Really are the Worst Traveller

On our way to Oklahoma, I'm driving my jeep.
After our first road trip together I never trusted you to drive me long distance anywhere ever again.

I pulled over at a rest stop in Kansas. We were travelling with animals.

We'd just stopped to make a quick trip to let the dog use the restroom. I was headed inside to use the bathroom. I left the car running, and specifically told you to take the keys with you when you took the dog out for a walk.

With an annoyed tone you said "Yeah. Got it. I'm not a child, you don't have to remind me to do every little thing."

I make it halfway to the bathroom when I hear a blood curdling scream and cursing.

It was you.

You left the car running and locked the keys inside the car.

Neglecting the need to empty my bladder, I run back to try and soothe you.

To coddle you like an infant.

You wouldn't stop screaming.

Yanking the dog around on the leash while doing so. People were starting to stare.

I was calmly asking you to keep quiet.

You were drawing attention to us.

Like every one of your other public meltdown episodes.

Why do I love you? I can't stand you. I have to do everything.

While you continued to scream and throw a tantrum, I called 911 to let them know there was a cat locked inside our running vehicle at a rest stop. The temperature outside was below freezing. They sent over the only locksmith in the nearby town.

We were in the middle of nowhere Kansas and it only took 25 minutes for them to arrive. It was a sweet young couple in an older pickup truck. They said it was $50 to unlock the car and they were cash only. I agreed; I knew I had cash in the car-Just wasn't sure how much.

It took them two minutes to unlock it and I was so, so thankful.

I searched for my money and all I had was $25. I had food, gifts for my family, and offered anything else I had to them. They declined and didn't seem bothered at all. They took only the $25 and said Merry Christmas.

What did Augustin do? Absolutely nothing. Just stood by with a sour look on his face and that notorious dead gaze in his eyes. I wish I could've left him at the rest stop and driven to Oklahoma alone.

I solved our issue—the issue that he created, in less than an hour.

While he did nothing.

He never even said thank you to the kind strangers that helped us, or to me for finding a solution while he cried and screamed like a child.

Astral Connection

We'd had this odd connection for months now.
We seemed to be able to read each other.
Even when we weren't in the vicinity of one another.
I remember feeling hot at work.
Angry for no reason.
My cheeks burning.

It was near the end of my shift and I drove home to the studio we shared.
Soon after I get in you tell me Gemma came over for closure.
She came over and you sat in her car to talk. Gave her some mail the she'd had sent to the shop.
I screamed.

I ripped my own shirt straight down the middle.
You stayed calm while I lost control for once.
It wasn't the fact that she came over for closure that bothered me.
It's the fact that you two were able to meet. Give one another closure. Hug.
Say goodbye.
If it were me?

Not a fucking chance.

I couldn't have male friends. Couldn't hang out with Stacey without you thinking I would "talk about you behind your back" when I was with her.

But I'm supposed to take this news and act like you deserve any action other than aggressive behavior?

When my mom and brother came to visit I didn't get more than 3 hours alone with them.

You wanted me on a tight leash.

Which is comical, since the aggressive bitch in this relationship is you.

At a Stoplight

This is our routine.

I mention how I don't like the way you talk to me, the way you make me feel.

You tell me I only focus on the negative.

Like I'm in a red room.

Developing photos that apparently don't exist to you.

But they're here.

Black and white.

They say if you take a picture, a moment will last longer.

Most of our arguments seemed to be photos.

They never seemed to disappear.

Permanent once fully developed.

Every new argument seemed to bring up the photos of our past.

I can't stand it any longer. I jumped out of the car at a stoplight and headed for the other direction.

Later on you told me this gave you flashbacks of Nicole and Gemma.

They'd also jumped out of cars just to get away from you.

A decade of the same patterns.
The same photos.

You'd think you'd change the constant rather than the variable to produce a different result.
But that's not how your world works.
Since it literally revolves around you.

It Wasn't The Dog

I'll never forget the time I came home from work. We'd had one of our notorious fights earlier that morning. I came home to see my baby blanket—the one my grandmother hand sewed for me before I was born; torn to unrecognizable shreds. It was placed on our papasan chair; which isn't where I'd left it.

I was immediately overrun with shock and asked you what happened-my eyes wide.

I could always tell when you were lying.

I just wanted to hear what you had to say this time.

You looked at me with a false sense of surprise on your face and had the audacity to say " Oh nooo, it must've been Mr. Loggs" (The dog)

I asked you why the blanket wasn't where I had left it. I always kept my blanket put away, safe from the dangers of our environment.

You said you'd grabbed the blanket out of the chest and thrown it on the chair.

And told me "Mr. Loggs must have scratched it and torn it up trying to get cozy. I'm so sorry"

Now this is the part I'm sorry for. I wanted to make you sorry for what I knew YOU had done. This wasn't the work of the dog. I knew that. But I also knew if I accused you of what I knew YOU had done, and told you I was hurt, it would just start another endless argument that ended in tears.

The next part here breaks my heart, and I'm still sorry to this day.

Mr. Loggs didn't deserve this. But I knew hurting him would be the only way to make you understand the absolute betrayal and hurt I was feeling.

I open palm backhanded the little dog right in his innocent face. Imagining it was you.

Absolutely reveling in your shock.

Your feeling of guilt.

I could see these emotions on your sick, twisted face.

Screaming obscenities at the dog that were meant for you.

You put your hand over your mouth and your eyes seemed to wilt. You actually softened for once.

This was one of the few times in this relationship where I felt in control. Like I had power.

To this day I'm still sorry for what I did to the dog. But not sorry for how it broke your heart.

It Started Out Consensual

We were being intimate in the loft upstairs.
The ambient glow of string lights above our heads.
Everything started out as normal.
With kissing, caressing.
I could tell something was off.

While you were on top of me you abruptly tore your lips away from mine and had a look of rage in your eyes.

You rolled over and said in disgust "WHY am I always the one to initiate sex" "It's like you don't even want me" "It's not my responsibility to make the first move all the time"

I asked what the hell your problem was and you began raising your voice.

Talking nonsense about how you don't feel wanted.

Those feelings would've been valid, if we weren't already naked and getting intimate with each other.

That should've been a conversation fully clothed.
Sitting across from one another.
Speaking to each other at a normal volume.

We briefly argued back and forth.

Still naked.

And I told you to just finish.

You angrily jumped back on top of me, even more enraged than before

And started slamming yourself into me.

I don't even remember the words you were spitting through your teeth at that point.

I just remember how low they made me feel.

Hands pinned above my head, the string lights above me now a winding blur because of your hate-filled abrupt motions.

You finish in 2 minutes.

You roll off of me and we don't speak the rest of the night.

Lights out until tomorrow morning.

The morning after was silent.

I wish there was a pill for this.

Lunch With Sam

You closed the shop for lunch and invited Sam and I to get a rack of ribs near the shop. I liked being included on these little outings.

Having Sam around always seemed to influence you to be nicer to me.

We'd gotten our food and sat down at a nearby table. There were canvassers standing outside the store asking people to sign their petition to make college free for American citizens.

You said no, you wouldn't sign it, and rudely made a comment about how you had to pay for college, so why shouldn't other people.

They asked Sam and I next if we were registered. Sam wasn't but I was. I ended up saying I wasn't. I wanted to sign the petition because I believed in the cause. But I didn't feel like arguing with Augustin. He shortly left to go to the bathroom and I confessed to Sam I wanted to sign it.

He told me, "Ivy, you have to start doing things for yourself. You need to stand up for what you believe in"

Another little gem that's burned into my memory.

Thanks Sam.

Where'd You Hide My Drugs

This has to be the worst memory of you.

The magnum opus of your meltdowns.

You'd been out late and told me you'd be back at a certain time.

Hours had gone by after your projected return. This was a codependent relationship. I know that now.

I was actually concerned for your safety. You'd already been to jail once during our relationship. I thought maybe this would be another one of those times.

I called your parents and asked if you were over at their place. Out of genuine concern.

Wrong move.

You get home shortly after. I can tell by the look on your face this was going to be a terrible night.

This was the big one.

Without hesitation. Without saying hello. You start yelling at me. "WHY THE FUCK DID YOU CALL MY PARENTS?!"

"I just got a call from my dad asking where the fuck I was."

I tried to explain I was worried about where you were.

You completely took this out of context.

You accused me of accusing you of cheating.

The thought didn't even cross my mind.

You're an angry, manipulative hot-head that can't control his temper even in public.

The thought of you going to jail for one of your famous outbursts was a real possibility.

You wouldn't stop screaming at me.

Next you went to the bookshelf and cracked open a book on the top shelf.

With a wild glare on your face we lock eyes.

This is the loudest I've heard you yell.

"WHERE THE FUCK ARE MY DRUGS? WHERE THE FUCK DID YOU PUT THEM."

You threw the book across the room.

I had no idea what you were talking about. You stomp over to me and get half an inch away from my face and scream the same question over and over.

I start crying and try to get away from you.

I tell you I don't even know what you're talking about.

You won't stop screaming and digging through books looking for god knows what.

You keep accusing me.

This isn't going to end. I've never seen you like this.

I made an executive decision to gather my backpack and try to head out the door.

You grab my backpack and pull me down to the floor.

I'm screaming as loud as I can at this point.

Please-- neighbors, bystanders, anyone listening, PLEASE someone call for help.

I get away from you and run out the door to my car. I start the engine as fast as I can and start driving away. I just had to get away from you, drive around the corner and decide where to go.

Stacey.

My only friend at this point.

I'd pushed everyone else away for you.

I called her panting, and asked if I could stay the night. You were going insane.

Of course she said yes. She wasn't even home but her roommate was. He let me in and I had a good night's rest at Stacey's.

When I'm getting settled into her bed it's already midnight.

You call me. I decline.

You call again. Again. Again.

I can't even set my alarm because you won't stop calling me.

I have work in the morning.

I can't do this.

I have my phone on airplane mode now.

Peace.

I can get a good nights rest at least.

Morning comes and unfortunately I turn airplane mode off.

43 text messages.

That's a new record for you.

In the messages you called Stacey a whore. Called me one too. Said we were both stupid. Told me to not come home.

I'd left so quickly the night before I didn't even grab a change of clothes or a toothbrush.

I had to get ready for work but I needed my things.

I head back to the home we shared.

It's quiet. You're awake but I can't engage right now.

I head back to the room where I kept my things and open the door.

Pure destruction.

My clothes are all over the floor.

Everything has been pulled out of the closet. Scattered EVERYWHERE.

The paintings on the wall had been broken.

You slashed my sister's painting with a knife right down the middle.

Lucio Fontana style.

You ripped pages out of my books.

Tore letters from my father to shreds.

Dumped out all of my sentimental boxes. Stomped on all the items in there.

The entire house was spotless-- but my room?

Ransacked. By you.

I'm in shock. Silently screaming and tears running down my face. I still had to get ready for work.

I pick up a clean shirt from the floor.

A fresh pair of socks.

Still crying I head to the bathroom to get ready.

You tell me you'll fix this.

I will myself to go to work. An empty shell. I can't even recall how the day was.

Coming back home you had most of my things cleaned up.

The clothes back in the closet.

The paintings though? Destroyed. And that hurts the most.

You told me your parents came over and saw the mess you created.

That's when they decided they'd pay for you to go to anger management.

A glimmer of hope.

They see it too. I'm not crazy.

Please, please, let this work.

Destroying My Sister's Paintings

After the fiasco where you pinned me down and screamed at me-- asking where I hid your drugs and decided to destroy everything in my room after I had escaped to Stacey's,

I told you I expected you to fix the paintings for free. You said of course you would.

One of the canvas paintings had a complete tear right down the middle. The other one was a wooden piece a friend had painted for me. Completely broken in half.

The pieces that you broke sat in your frame shop for 3 months. Untouched.

Your friend Kara comes in with a couple of projects that she needed framed and you finished those up for her in a week. Even gave her a little discount.

Funny how the paintings you destroyed are still sitting in the corner.

No plans to be repaired.

Now this is a fight that I started. I asked you why that bitch's artwork got framed and sent out the door before you even started working on repairing my paintings.

Finally you said sorry. Yet another time you were speechless.

You had no excuse. And this victory felt incredible.

That's what our relationship became.

A constant battle between two disgruntled lovers.

Repeatedly disappointing the other and taking notes.

A few weeks later you had me come back into the shop to take a look at the finished product. I could still see the knife mark in my sister's canvas painting. But yes, it looked much better hot glued back together. The wooden painting? You had to frame it in two pieces, since you'd broken a solid wood piece in half. The frames didn't even match. I could tell you just used extra material you had leftover from other orders. I don't even like silver.

They looked tacky.

You left the wood working room to go up to the front and help a customer. It was just Sam and I in the back. His comment to me was: " About time those got fixed, isn't it?"

This comment made my heart melt. It was such a simple comment but it let me know he thought what

Augustin did, and how he prioritized everyone else's work over my sentimental paintings was wrong.

Thank you Sam.

Pit Stop In New Mexico

This was on our way back from the Grand Canyon.

You wanted to drive through New Mexico and stop at a few of your favorite spots.

Spic and Span. A cute diner that was famous for their cream puff pastries. Your grandmother loved them.

We were already arguing when we sat down.

My tone wasn't right when I asked you a question.

Something stupid and minuscule.

The usual.

After we'd eaten we get back in the car. You're talking about stopping to visit your family's land that they have out there.

You were excited. We were talking about tiny home living. Eco living. Starting a farm together. Working on art in the middle of nowhere.

Somewhere between talking about the possibility of a future together you snapped.

You said maybe we shouldn't go.

The last person you brought there was Gemma.

You worked on art together in a field.

You told me this place was sacred. You didn't want to bring me here if we were fighting.

Funny how your family spaces are sacred and you respect that.

But when we're around my family you don't have a problem embarrassing me.

Silent screaming in the grocery store.

Stomping right past my mother in the airport because we were fighting.

Dumping out my suitcase at my family reunion to look for rolling papers.

Utter disrespect.

Fuck your land.

Don't take me to your vacant field. I don't need to go there.

I already experience enough emptiness being with you.

Tom's Cabin

Another "sacred" place to you.

Tom had invited us to his parents' cabin in the mountains.

Before we'd even gotten on the highway we had started fighting at a Japanese restaurant.

The fight was about how you respond when I bring up the way you talk to me. How you always raise your voice and interrupt me.

And what did you do for half of the car ride?

Continued to interrupt me. Told me I always bring up the past.

When actually--

I'm exposing a pattern.

Making it to the cabin, tensions are eased when Tom invites us in.

How could they not be?

It seems all your friends are level-headed and non-argumentative.

One would think if you surrounded yourself with people like this, you would absorb at least some of their characteristics.

Fortunately, the entire weekend at the cabin we didn't fight.

As soon as there's another person in the mix, you seem to treat me like a normal person.

Alone, behind closed doors; a different story

The First Time I Said "I Hate You"

At this point does it even matter what the fight was about?

We seemed to have the same one over and over.

Every fight you ALWAYS talked over me. Interrupted me. I could NEVER defend myself and as soon as I would open my mouth you would smash my words with yours.

I felt something different in my chest.

My tolerance of your behavior hanging on by a thread.

Scars on my face from scratching myself.

Scabs on my temples from nervously picking at my skin.

I'm exhausted. Exhausted from living a life like this.

We can't go a single week without fighting. I've been keeping tally marks.

Like I'm in prison.

All I hear is you yelling and I can't take it anymore. I walk towards the bathroom and lock myself in.

Sitting on the toilet with my hands over my ears.

Please god I just need some peace.

Please make him go away.

Please help him understand I'm trying to remove myself from the situation. I can't do this anymore.

He's banging on the door now. Jiggling the handle. I can hear him screaming even with my ears covered.

I press my hands as hard as I can into my head and hold my breath.

Nope. I still hear the screaming.

I needed out. But god I can't leave this bathroom. This 5x5 room is my only safe haven.

As loud as I could, not even recognizing my voice.

This came from deep within my gut. This was real.

"I HATE YOU. I HAAAATE YOOOOU."

That's when I put my foot through the door.

I kicked not one hole in the door, but two.

Great.

Now I added another fight onto this one.

I ruined the door.

I said something you should never say to your partner.

This is turning into an all night event.

I can't stay in the bathroom all evening.

You're in a full-blown rage at this point.

Eventually I open the door and tell you I'm done for the night.

I head upstairs to try and get some rest. I feel like I'm going to faint.

This doesn't stop you. You start kicking objects around the room. Doing your signature move of walking around in circles and cursing.

One thing I did right tonight?

I located a pair of earplugs and shoved them as far as I could in my ear canal.

I could still hear you screaming. Mr. Loggs was terrified and came running up the stairs with me. Tail tucked between his legs.

This poor sweet baby. He gets under the covers with me and we're each other's comfort for the night.

I wake up in the morning and see that you're not next to me.

You're downstairs. The next thing I see?

Writing.

All over the walls.

Written on the wall over and over are the words : I hate you. She hates me. Whore. Whore. Whore. Over and over. Covering the perimeter. All the way up to the ceiling.

You ran out of room and even went through the trouble of standing on a step stool to write even higher.

I'm speechless.

WHAT THE FUCK DID YOU DO?

You were actually calm. You actually looked sorry this time.

I start tearing up and you came to comfort me. Said things like "I know. I'm so sorry, I'm so sorry I'll fix this."

How did you fix it?

You invited a couple of your friends over to help you paint over it.

I'm glad they saw it. I'm glad they caught a glimpse of the person you can be.

I don't think it made any difference though.

But it made me happy.

Made me feel less insane.

Swerving Toward a Man on a Bike

This was during the time my friend Courtney and her husband were visiting. You had driven me to the Denver art museum and they were going to meet us there. By the time they were up and ready to meet us the museum only had 30 minutes left until they closed and weren't letting people in. You were disappointed they'd made us wait for them to get there. We're headed toward I-25 about to cross the turquoise bridge on Speer blvd. We had a joint lit and were smoking in the car while driving.

A man on a commuter bike glanced over as you were taking a drag. I guess he looked at you the wrong way.

The next second you swerved. Hard.

Aggressively toward him.

Jolting me sideways in my seat.

Making the seatbelt restrict my entire body; the material digging into my neck.

I asked what the fuck you thought you were doing.

Your exact answer?

"Fuck him and his bike. I didn't like the way he looked at me"

I'm so embarrassed to be seen with you.

Complete strangers aren't even safe from your wrath.

Down Low At Lowdown

I'd received a gift card to a restaurant for doing well at work.

I'd decided I wanted to have lunch with you.

We sit down and order drinks.

Minor small talk is had.

The waiter comes over to take our order.

He turns to me first and before telling them what I'd like to eat, I simply said, "This will be separate tickets by the way"

Paying for my own food was the only way for me to maintain an ounce of independence from you.

Immediately your face does that thing where it goes cold.

Personality number 2 sets in.

What did I even do this time?

The waiter takes your order next and as soon as he turns his back you're reprimanding me for embarrassing you.

According to you it's classless to ask the waiter to separate the checks before we order.

This ruined the entire meal. You wouldn't let it go.

Didn't smile once.

We continued to argue.

About what?

We ate in silent discontent.

When the check finally came I slid my gift card back into my wallet and pulled out cash to pay for my half of the meal.

You immediately noticed and said "Oh, now you're gonna save that for another time? Okay, have fun with another one of your hoes"

You always loved projecting your insecurities onto me.

I responded with "I'll be coming here alone, when you're not here to ruin it for me. Not going to waste my reward on your attitude."

Wrong thing to say.

We went to bed without speaking to each other.

Any and every action I take produces a negative result from you.

Unwillingly Having Sex With You To Maintain This Relationship

During the worst part of our relationship, a couple of months before our breakup, the thought of having sex with you made my skin crawl.

How am I supposed to be turned on by someone that makes me cry a minimum of 3 times a week, with a fight every other day?

Don't forget; I've been keeping tally marks at this point.

Every time you crawled on top of me, I'd disassociate.

What kept me going? The thought of Sam. When he'd join us for drinks after work.

The way his laugh sounded. His stories.

The quiet way he'd give me an understanding glance letting me know he was still listening to me while I was talking. Even when you'd start talking over me.

The thought of someone respecting me and saying kind words became a fantasy.

I wanted his brown eyes looking back at me. Not yours.

Its incredible how the mind can create Edenic scenes that transcend the physical realm.

I kept this up for months.

When I Found Your Relationship Journal

This was after you'd destroyed most of my sentimental items.

Presents from my parents.

Books from my grandparents with sweet notes.

You'd ripped the pages out.

I wanted to destroy something of yours while you were at work.

I was left alone in the studio.

Seething.

I see the painting your friend Miguel painted for you. His self-portrait. I felt blood rushing to my face and pleasure in my bones.

At the thought of knocking the painting off the wall.

Spitting on it.

And tearing it to shreds.

God that would be bliss.

But I didn't. Part of me regrets not doing it. But at least I can say I'm better than you.

I continued to look around the studio. Destroying computer equipment? Not good enough. Easily replaceable; especially with mommy and daddy's money.

It had to be something that meant a lot to you.

Rifling through a milk crate I find a black journal I'd never seen before.

I open it and it's a love journal between you and Gemma.

Gemmy Baby.

With cute little drawings. Recapping your days together. Love notes written by each of you, to one another.

After all the awful things you said about her, I'd wondered why you kept this.

I came across one of the last few pages.

A drawing of 3 peas in a pod.

A pregnancy announcement.

You were going to be a father. She was happy about it.

But there never came a baby.

You'd mentioned before that you had an ex that had an abortion.

But this? Wow.

Announcing that you were about to be a father.

And then aborting the fetus.
Child. Son or daughter.
Whatever you called it.
And you held onto this?

I had something tangible in my hands now that I could destroy.

Something if I destroyed, would in turn destroy you.

I tore every single one of those pages into tiny shreds.

Placed the journal back where I'd found it.

I held onto the shredded pages for months.

Waiting for the right time.

And I certainly found that moment.

It was one of our last few fights.

Right after we'd broken up. Not even 24 hours had passed and you had all of my possessions placed outside of the studio.

This was it. I'd been keeping the shredded pages in my car.

I calmly go out to grab them and waltz back in.

I open the studio door and fling every single one of them at your head.

Your face drops. Turns to stone. And I walk out.

This was the best I'd felt around you in a long time.

We loved to inundate each other with hate.
This was our love language.

The Night of Crush Walls

You and I had split up at this point. Doing that ridiculous thing that couples do when they break up; meeting up for a casual night out. Sam was there. As usual, to be the mediator.

Before even seeing any of the murals or artwork, we'd decided to get a bite to eat at a nearby pizza place. We all sit down, order, and chat as normal. This feels good. I'm maintaining hope that we can get back to our friendship as it had started in the beginning. The beginning where we'd stay up late smoking spliffs and just talking, listening to music. Or taking a trip to tunnel two and watching the stars.

Wasn't gonna happen. Especially this night. Sam had a friend to meet so he went around the corner to meet up with them. Leaving just you and I at the table. Big fucking mistake.

Within 3 minutes of him leaving, you ask me "What're we doing? Why the fuck are you here" I'm confused as to what this is" I tell you I thought we were trying to return to how we treated each other in the beginning. Getting back to our friendship first before continuing a relationship. I can't recall what was said next but it ended in me leaving your hateful ass at the table all alone and running away.

I'm running around a few blocks, taking random turns here and there hoping you wouldn't follow me.

Sam sees me running and calls out to me. He yells my name and out of anger for Augustin…and maybe a little for him since he left Augustin and I alone, I screamed "FUCK YOU" right back to him and kept running.

You know when you lie in bed at night and think of all the things in life you regret?

This is one of those things I've done that I regret. Truly embarrassed by this.

Sam didn't deserve my projected anger.

Sorry Sam.

Butts And Trumpets

After all the negative-yet true stories.
I'd like to mention one thing I don't think I'll find anywhere else.

A shared moment between two people forever.

Chaotic and never meant to be re-created.

Sitting in a swivel chair as I usually did in the studio.

You'd been working on a painting for a while.

Tacked up on the wall nearest to the bathroom you were improv painting.

Black paint marker in hand, you asked me what to draw next.

I said butts.

You easily draw a few butts here and there.

Next I tell you to draw trumpets.

Without hesitation you start drawing a trumpet protruding from two butt cheeks.

Later on you draw a shoe coming out of another butt.

The entire canvas covered in butts and objects coming out of the butts.

I witnessed the majority of the painting being brought to life.

You filled in the outline of the trumpet with gold.

The shoe you painted green.

I didn't make a single mark on this canvas but I felt empowered by it.

Like it was one of the few times you actually heard my voice and weren't annoyed with what I was saying.

The painting; as campy as it was, brought me comfort.

Later you hung it in the shop and every time I'd pass by I felt like it was our secret.

This giant piece of art must have some meaning behind it. People attempting to interpret it.

But only I knew the true significance behind the work.

The Last Time I Saw You

We'd tried to be friends.
 I came to your art show. I was in it, actually.
We were cordial. I'd spent the night with you.
No sex.

A few days after you came to my apartment. We just talked. Smoked weed.

You were there maybe 30 minutes.

Halfway into our spliff.

You're sitting across from me.

I'm standing in the kitchen.

I can't remember our conversation, but I remember your actions.

I took a single glance at my stove—-to make sure I hadn't left it on. Because I do that frequently.

You interpreted this action as me looking at the clock. Counting time.

Ushering you to go---insinuating it was late and you needed to leave.

Absolutely not what I was doing whatsoever.

The next words out of your angry, thin lipped mouth?

"IF YOU WANT ME TO LEAVE JUST SAY SO. I'M NOT TRYING TO WASTE YOUR TIME."

Since we weren't together at this point, it lit a fire inside me unlike any prior to this moment.

I was free.

Gaining my strength, dignity, and self-respect back.
I was strong enough to leave you.
Kind enough to think we could be friends.
This was a new level of disrespect.
I don't have to go home with you.
We no longer live together.
I won't be sleeping next to you tonight.
This knowledge empowers me.

In an angry whisper through gritted teeth I told you to get the fuck out of my house.

I never wanted to see you again.

You leave and finally I get to slam a door, shutting you out permanently.

I had you blocked on every social media platform.

When you figured out you couldn't get through to me, you decided to send an email my way.

You emailed a message telling me I was worse than Gemma now.

That I deserve nothing good in my life.

You told me to keep wearing my whore makeup. That you never wanted to see me again.

Ensuring that you had the final word.

Pathetic.

PART TWO

WATER

Normalize Love

Not romantic love between two people
But love for other people throughout the world

Love for random moments and glances shared with a stranger

Love for those vacation relationships that may have only lasted 5 days

Love for your hostel mates that bought you a drink or were just passing through

Love for a stranger you met outside of a train station

We watched the sunrise together and never saw each other again

Love for Hanne, the host that allowed me to stay in her home while I volunteered abroad

Love for the first relationship I had that wasn't abusive

It still ended, but I still loved it

I never would've been on a boat under the Golden Gate Bridge awestruck by its magnificence if we hadn't met

Honestly a once in a lifetime experience

Love for the person you trained at work

That ended up becoming one of your closest friends and roommate

Love for the girl that allowed you to stay with her while you left your abusive relationship

Our friendship may have ended

But my love for what she did to help me will never die

Love for moments forever held in time and in the depths of your subconscious

Certain scents and sounds will resurrect these moments when you least expect them

It's one of the purest forms of love

Even without family, friends, or a partner, you'll have these random memories that remain with you to make their presence known when you need them the most

It's love, Love

Strangers to Neighbors

Since I moved into the studio in the back of my partner's shop, (It was a modified apartment in the back of a commercial building)

I didn't have any neighbors.

I was subject only to his explosive company.

I'd isolated myself from all of my friends and had no way to make any new ones.

At the time I worked as an interior gardener.

I would work downtown visiting roughly 50 different offices on a weekly basis.

All of them filled with people living intricate lives of their own.

You start to see the same people week after week.

Most don't even notice you're in the office.

But each office would have a select few individuals that would strike up a conversation with me.

Sometimes I'd learn incredibly personal details about these people's lives.

I'd heard about divorces, shopping addictions, family troubles, and their travels.

I congratulated people and shared in their elation when they showed me photos of a house they just bought or a wedding engagement.

I shared frustrations when people were unhappy at work or stressed about life's hardships.

I even had a woman voice her concern to me about possibly getting fired.

She was an insomniac and hadn't been doing so well at work.

Next week her desk was empty and I never saw her again.

These interactions were the most normal I'd experience each week.

It was always chaotic at home.

Every week I looked forward to going to work and started dreading the weekends.

The kindness and vulnerability they shared with me kept me sane.

These people became my neighbors, even though I didn't have a place of my own.

Reverse Pick-Pocket

On the verge of another breakdown, I was weak from the horrendous relationship I was trapped in. My credit card information had recently been stolen and it was going to be a few days before I'd get any money back.

Determined not to ask my partner for any help, I was working on becoming independent from our codependency.

My plan of action after work was to steal some cat food from a convenience store. Today was the day I needed to restock and dead set on not having to ask for help, I decided it was better to steal.

I was working downtown watering plants.

Toward the end of my shift I'd hopped off the bus and a strange man walks up to me.

He asks if he can reverse pick-pocket me and I thought at first he was mentally ill.

He further explained that he'd like to give me a handful of single dollar bills. He called it a reverse pick-pocket because he was giving money away to strangers.

I took it with hesitation, but started tearing up and said thank you. I told him I'd be buying food for my cat with it and that I really needed it that day.

He told me he could feel my gratitude and said to pay it forward one day if I ever could.

I didn't even catch his name.

Heather Love

We'd met in high school.

She and my friends were of the few that would spend their lunch hour in the library.

I remember the first time she'd shown us her "Random Thoughts" journal.

It was pocket sized and she'd carry it with her everywhere.

She influenced my friend Haley and I to start one as well.

A decade later, I'm able to compile some of those thoughts into this book.

I'd be wrong to say she wasn't a major inspiration for my journey with writing.

There aren't any other stories about her, but she designed the blueprint for what you're reading today.

A decade ago I remember her quietly journaling these random thoughts.

She moved away the next year.

The most influential people in my life never seem to stay for long.

Currently she lives in South Korea and teaches there for work.

I no longer carry around a small paper pocket notebook and instead, whenever random thoughts or excerpts creep up, I pull out my phone and speak my notes into a piece of technology instead.

Every new saved note in my phone is laced with the faint memory of her.

Thank you, for the continued creative revelations.

The World Shows Me Its Secrets Because It Knows I Can Keep Them

My second trip heading to Alaska
I found this flower (Scottish thistle) above the check-in kiosk.

I figured it to be a symbol of safe travels—as I was nervous to be flying alone so far away.

I placed it between the pages of the book I was carrying and made my way toward the departure gate.

I sat next to a man with a shaven head and glasses, wearing a verdigris shirt.

I opened the book to commence reading and the man next to me took notice of the flower, and asked if I had found it at the check in kiosk.

Of course I said yes.

He went on to tell me he had picked it for his wife; it was her favorite flower.

This wasn't just a ploy to talk to me either.

He lifted up his shirt to show me the tattoo on his chest, with the flower permanently inked on his skin; the name "Michelle" written under it.

Smiling, I tried giving it back.

He said "No, it was meant for you to find and keep."

Out of all the people I could've sat next to, all the airlines and kiosks used for check in, my pattern of motion matched his completely.

Two strangers shared a moment of synchronicity.

As it was time to board my flight, while standing in line I took one last glance at the man I'd just shared this anomaly with, and he was staring back at me.

Clearly still marveling at the oddity.

Our eyes locked and we gave each other a grin as if to say

"Goodbye Forever"

Strange Woman In A Strange Land

Never forget the strange woman
    Sitting across the table from you

Her eyes- a mute periwinkle

A woman you met 3 days ago, telling you to never get married

That this isn't a woman's purpose

Finally

An elder woman who doesn't view my young beautiful existence as a "prize" for my future husband to inseminate

But remember your own grandmother telling you with haste: "You're going to need to learn how to change diapers, because you'll have to do this one day"

Even today when I call her, I never get asked about my goals or ambition

I spent two weeks with this strange woman

We'd made dinner for one another and spent time in the garden

She was 73 years old at the time living alone in a beautiful house

Dried hydrangeas hanging in the corner of the kitchen window

This massive amethyst crystal lying askew on the oak table

The marionettes in another corner hanging lifeless

With hand stitched leather shoes and shards of broken glass where their eyes should have been

She shared stories with me about her time as a nurse

About her previous marriage and journey with finding independence

She did yoga regularly and her house was filled with books

I have a specific memory of her standing in her garden near the medicine wheel

Just acknowledging how beautiful the day was

And she said with delight "Everything is perfect, all the time"

I did nothing more than admire the positivity she exuded

I can't recall ever meeting anyone so inspiring and open-minded

A complete stranger on a different continent became a permanent inspiration and I dream of her and the house that overlooks the water often

Her memory is forever burned into my psyche and one of the best decisions I've ever made was volunteering abroad to stay with her

Pacing Wires

I always remembered the man that told me getting the pacing wires taken out of my body feels a bit like falling in love.

He didn't mention that it was agonizing pain.

It literally took the breath out of me.

I felt stunned.

It wasn't until years later I realized what he said was inherently plausible.

It's exactly what falling in love feels like.

What he failed to mention was, it feels like unrequited love.

Sitting there jaded after the procedure I felt betrayed by this stranger.

Like he blatantly lied to me.

Nearly a decade later I had a moment of clarity and smiled to myself.

This stranger coyly warned me about the torment one experiences with falling in love, while simultaneously easing my anxiety about the pain of the procedure that lie ahead.

Not a Match

Date after date and no one even begins to compare to you.

I've never been able to recreate the excitement of meeting another person.

An unspoken esoteric meeting of two souls that I continue trying to regurgitate.

The people are nice. Handsome.

But they don't have your voice.

Like a match I try striking a single conversation that mimics our hundreds of previous ones.

A spark is never created and although there's ample kindling, the fire never begins.

Trying to keep warm by a fire that is never started is indescribably cold and isolating.

Ali

Wherever we were created
    In nothingness we sat with our backs to one another completely attached
    We could feel and we could hear
    But we couldn't see each other

    We wanted more from this tangible existence
    The pursuit of sight led us to detach and walk in opposite directions from ourselves

    We vowed that with our separation, we would be blessed with the gift of seeing each other completely for the first time

    We spent lifetimes walking straight ahead
    Having separate experiences
    Leaving footprints of misery, gratitude, elation, and loss

    Until one day
    We finally meet again at the starting point
    But this time we face each other
    For the first time without ever seeing you

I recognize you immediately

Your dark eyes prompt memories of a serpent I'd seen in a life before

I'm the tail of the snake
And you're its mouth
I willingly place myself inside the shadow of your existence as you continue to swallow me whole

Our reunion an ouroboros
Enveloped in darkness where I began in the void
This is home
The beginning and end

Reza

How can I forget the hours we spent sitting across from one another on your sofa.

Every time I visit---sometimes months apart; your apartment is always the same.

Everything has its place.

The plants above your fireplace.

The religious deity on top of your fridge.

Two paper planes on a side table in the corner.

Living room window wide open.

Usually we share a bowl of fruit over our chat.

Once it was pomegranate-- another time black cherries.

A little bit of sake.

Hours we sit looking at one another's faces.

Your gentle voice responding to a question of mine.

Educated banter and memories shared between us.

Sometimes I feel like your therapist.

And I like it.

I feel wanted; like you need me here.

Who else would listen?

Even if another person listened, would they respond accordingly?

We speak in tandem.

No awkward pauses.

Only eloquent sentences pouring from our mouths into each other's ears.

I've been waiting to meet you.

And always sad to leave your place.

It's been a lifetime since we've seen each other.

When we reunite we melt into the other.

Mauricio

I traveled solo to Tulum and the first night wrote a sad excerpt about eating alone at the same place where Paul and I had once shared a meal at MEZE. That same night I gathered cranberry juice from a local convenience store and decided to drink alone in my hostel until I passed out.

Loneliness creeping in. With Covid I was expecting to have the entire Hostel to myself. Around 11PM I hear the door handle jingle. I open it and see Mauricio for the first time. I'd accidentally locked him out without knowing I'd done so. That first night we spent the night talking and listening to music on the rug; his friend Charley also accompanying us. It was one of the first real human connections I'd had in a long time.

He asked me out to breakfast. We spent every day on the beach together. Every night together. Another morning he woke me up by reaching his hand up to my bunk and reached for mine; we locked hands for a few seconds. I climbed down my bunk ladder and spent the morning just cuddling with him.

When they left, I felt the void returning inside my chest. I was alone again. I tried going to the beach, sitting on the cabanas and gazing at the ocean. It was great; but again, I just felt empty once more.

I had multiple people approach me and try to start a conversation. None of them interested me. Talking to them actually made me feel more isolated. I ended up injuring myself very badly by falling down a flight of stairs and busted my knee. I could barely walk. I was clambering down the stairs the next morning to ask the hostel managers to order me a pair of crutches. They ordered them, but it was going to be about 3 hours before they even showed up. They had the private security guard walk me to a cabana and he brought me a bag of ice for my knee.

The next few days, the waiters at the beach club had come to know me pretty well. They sent a medic directly to my cabana to bandage me up and clean my wounds so they wouldn't get infected. After this day of constant help and empathy, I hobbled back to my room, struggling with haste to get up the flight of stairs.

I hear someone call to me and ask if I need help. I hate help. But god did I need it. His name was David and he was staying directly across from me, so he'd seen me struggling. He'd walked me up the steps directly to my door. He'd invited me out but I said I needed my leg to heal a bit more. The next morning here I am, hobbling back to the beach on my crutches-which by the way- were for a person that's 5'2". I'm 5'8". They were still helpful though and I was appreciative the hostel managers were able to order them for me. I couldn't stand not being able to get in the beautiful, turquoise water. So I did my best to creep over and soak my feet just a little.

A woman sitting on the beach called to me and asked what happened to my leg. I told her and she asked to pray over it. I'm not much into praying, but I knew she was asking to do this from a place of love; so I let her. She put her hands above my knee (Reiki style) and said a healing prayer for me.

Later in the afternoon I continue soaking in the sun, and a man walks up to me and asks what happened to my leg. He was selling bracelets on the beach and kneeled down to my level. His name was Tatan and he slid a tiger's eye bracelet over my wrist and wished for me to heal quickly. It was a short interaction but it was one of kindness. He walked away from me and continued selling bracelets along the beach. I never saw him again.

That same day I met a man from New York- a little boring in my opinion- but he'd also invited me out to dinner later. I'd told him no because my knee wasn't feeling good still. This man actually sent me the menu of a taco place and told me to pick something out and he delivered it directly to my hostel room later in the evening. I never heard from him after that.

My last night in Tulum, David- the man that helped me up the stairs- asked me to check out the DJ downstairs and go to a Kratom bar. My knee felt a bit better at this point so I went ahead and said yes.

We caught the sunset, which was pink and orange, with beams of light that seemed to protrude from one single cloud hanging over the pristine water. We went to our Kratom bar, checked out a cenote that we'd had all to ourselves, and had plenty of conversation. We had dinner later that night and ended it there. He helped me up the stairs one last time and we said goodbye forever.

I left the next morning and as I had my last breakfast while peering out at the white sand beach, I was overwhelmed by this inexplicable feeling of love and gratitude for all the strangers I'd met.

The man that helped me up the stairs with no expectations, the man that delivered food to my door, the waiters that helped me up and down the stairs, the bracelet man, and the woman that prayed over my knee—This was all love.

There's going to be so many times in this life when you feel empty and alone. This void that enters your chest that continues to make a return. But just like love, platonic and romantic; those feelings end eventually as well. Accept love where you can find it.

Mauricio was a romantic love-I felt excitement, the butterflies, and a connection. When he left, of course I felt a little sad but the world around me continued to show me so much love; just in a different way. Remember to keep your eyes open. Notice true kindness and love; it's always lurking somewhere. Even if it isn't the romantic version of love, people are generally trying to connect and make one another feel a little less alone.

Turbulence

On the plane ready to fly to Guadalajara
We had a rough takeoff
One bump and jerk after another
I began to grip the seat anxiously, steadying my breath with apprehension for the remainder of the flight

Glancing side to side I see no one else death-gripping the arm rests in their seats
Behind me I hear children laughing
I glance at the seats adjacent to me and see two children sitting next to whom I assume is their mother

With every bump, dip, and sound of possible mechanical failure, the children laugh gleefully
Getting more excited with each motion
Their mother in the aisle seat looks like me
The only person I see in my range of vision that's grasping the arm rests with their eyes closed, intermittently opening them

I can tell she's steadying her breathing
We locked eyes once she opened hers
Sharing the same frightened look, she says "I'm glad the kids are enjoying this"

I agreed with her and even through her mask, I could see she gave a slight smirk, and a worried eyebrow raise

Looking back at the woman and sharing her anxiety while simultaneously being soothed by the laughter and joy of her children, I felt safe

I sporadically recall this memory at different times during my life

I remember peering into this woman's eyes and sharing her fear

I felt appreciation for her carefree children that helped soothe the tension of the rocky flight

A band of three strangers assisted me in easing my greatest fears and I continue to think of them often

Moments like these I revisit with gratitude

A fleeting shared slice of time that I'll forever recall and have appreciation for

New Years In Guadalajara

Mauricio, the man I'd met in Tulum and spent 5 days with invited me to visit him in Guadalajara for the New Year. He was currently on a trip so I actually made it to his place before he did.

After 5 days of knowing each other he trusted me to let myself into his place. Full trust in each other, and trust in the people around me in a place I'd never been before.

I took a nap and he arrived a few hours later.

We'd spent a few days together and for New Years I was invited to have dinner with his family.

They'd welcomed me as though they'd known me for years.

We shared wine and dinner and I experienced a new tradition I'd never heard of.

Everyone at the table was given a bowl of 12 grapes. At midnight we would all take turns eating a single grape one at a time and saying out loud our wishes for the New Year. One for each month.

I'd flown to Guadalajara a couple of times after and we'd taken a road trip to the state of Nayarit. I'd seen places I never would've known if I hadn't met this person on a solo trip; If I never had trust in this person after knowing them for less than a week.

Later he'd even flown to Portland and we met up to spend a few more days together.

I'd never had any expectation that the relationship would go any farther than just enjoying one another's company. I think when we hold onto the expectation that acts of love need to develop further, we're stunting our own growth. It's enlightening to let go of certain expectations and just enjoy the small moments you have with people.

Damien

We'd met shortly after my breakup while at work.
Your first week on the job and I was training you.

We'd shared typical niceties between one another but then we started talking about toxicity in relationships.

I'd told you about how I would self-harm just to be able to speak.

Living everyday plagued by lethargy and a fleeting will to live.

You'd shared some of your stories with me and we created a more intimate connection through trauma bonding.

I felt cradled, knowing I wasn't the only one who experienced such an intense hate-filled relationship.

The more people I talked to, the more I realized this is a common occurrence.

We'd spent months as friends and ended up moving in together.

After multiple failed roommate situations, this one was unlike any other.

Years go by and he's become my best friend.

The person I can safely travel with.

We shared a mysterious experience in the Sand Dunes. We stayed out all night sand sledding. On the way back to the car it was pitch black and we saw 4 dark figures standing in a circle silently, as we walked right past them. They didn't look human.

It's possible they didn't exist, but since we both witnessed the figures, it's apparent we share an alchemical bond.

A year later I was in a long distance relationship at the time with someone that lived in San Francisco. It was Fleet Week and I'd been invited to hang out all weekend on a 1970s motor yacht. As soon as I was invited I suggested Damien tag along. I wanted my best friend there. Paul's parents thought it was odd I'd invited a friend for our weekend together, but most people don't understand the bond we share. He makes every experience more enjoyable.

The engine of the boat died on our last day as we were headed back to the marina.

We ended up having to get towed by another boat. Our flight back to Denver was in two hours and we needed to get there soon.

All of our luggage was already on the boat, so we ended up getting towed to a guest dock and in an iconic move, we both jumped off of this boat with our luggage like a couple of vagabonds and called an Uber to the airport from there.

Another time Paul, Damien, and I were tubing down Clear Creek in Golden. We all had our own floats, but after the third round Damien's was sliced open by a jagged rock. Floating ahead of him, I waited until I was in calmer waters to pull myself to the side of the bank and hop out. Walking along the bank I see him sitting alone on a rock. My float still in tact, we shimmy ourselves into it and float down the creek together.

He's helped me climb through a window when I was stuck on the ledge of an eight-story building, and I once woke up lying on only a top sheet with towels around me. Apparently I'd blacked out and vomited in my own bed. He cleaned me up, and gave me the sheets from his own bed so I wouldn't be cold.

We planned a trip to Miami together, but he would arrive a day earlier than me. He ended up losing his Air BnB last minute and wasn't getting refunded. High and dry, he called me crying while I was still in Denver, and without hesitation I gladly helped him out.

We can depend on each other when we're stranded or destitute, and there's never any air of judgment or attitude of inconvenience.

Often alone for the holidays, his family always invites me over and they've become a stand-in family, while mine is back home.

He's been the most reliable person in my life since I moved out of my parents' house.

He's my chosen family.

Our friendship never would have blossomed if I hadn't left Augustin, since having friends during our relationship proved to be difficult.

Staying in a poisonous relationship long after its expiry date forbids the possibility of experiencing true love—platonic or romantic.

Hold close the friends that lift you up, inspire you, and ones you can trust implicitly.

Parental Supervision

There's a plethora of people that experience toxicity within their own families.

Whether it's childhood abuse, continued verbal abuse throughout adulthood, or even being disowned, some of the first abusive relationships we experience can be within our own families.

I didn't experience direct abuse, but I was subjected to poisonous situations at a young age.

I feel like I've become a parent to my biological parents.

The angry childish father.

That lacks a true sense of self.

The mother that's had self esteem issues that have been apparent since as far back as I can remember.

The mother that has voiced her personal issues and concerns to you from a young age.

The mother that cries to you about being neglected by her own mother.

The mother that slit her wrist over the kitchen sink in a trance-like state.

I just remember the blood dripping down and a vague memory of a broken green glass.

I don't blame her for any of this. I actually identify with it.

Most parents spend their life trying to protect their children from the brutality of the world.

I feel like my responsibility now has been conserving or protecting the fragility of my mother against others.

My existence has become accepting my father will never change, and forcing myself to care for the person in front of me.

The father that complains to you about being alone during the holidays even though it's due to his own lack of planning and personal choices.

He threatens to start drinking again—A juvenile bluff.

Rather than getting defensive and personalizing every comment (the way he does)

I let him vent and remind myself he's never been able to handle his emotions and is hurting.

He's actually experienced a surplus of sadness throughout his life, so I try to be understanding.

The father that smashes electronics when he's angry.

His actions reminiscent of Augustin. I don't know how to act when he's like this.

The father that makes racial remarks and gets combative when I tell him to not say those things in my own house.

I pointed out to him the things he had said in my presence when I had visited only 2 years ago.

No apology. No ownership. Only arguing.

As I continue swimming in the uncharted waters of adulthood I've come to understand that my mother is a people pleaser, because her own mother rarely ever says anything nice to her.

She subconsciously seeks approval.

Since I was three years old I distinctly remember my grandmother insulting her intelligence. Calling her stupid. Making comments about her weight.

And it continues to this day.

She continues to defend her. Reminding me that my grandmother also had a rough childhood.

But it's not the child's responsibility to be the recipient of unhealed trauma.

After years of watching my mother struggle with depression and having an absent biological father, I'm filled with gratitude for the step-father that I was gifted.

The only chance I ever had at living a normal life was due to his presence.

He gave me my first example of true love outside of a family blood-line.

Having children from a previous marriage, he blessed me with siblings.

Provided for me as if I were his own.

My conscience is littered with sorrow for my birth parents.

My time spent with Augustin I felt I would be forever burdened with their curse. Destined to be subjected to poison for a lifetime. Unable to speak up.

Giving people multiple chances to hurt me time and time again.

It's my penultimate wish that my mother finds her voice one day and my father becomes proactive about managing his emotions.

I'm consumed with their internal torture.

I beg the void and the universe simultaneously that they are both graced with the same love I've experienced outside of family relationships.

Before their final sleep, I hope they gain the necessary assets to say goodnight to their pain.

I love you.

www.ingramcontent.com/pod-product-compliance
Lightning Source LLC
LaVergne TN
LVHW011844060526
838200LV00054B/4155